# Conditions of Work and Political Consciousness Among Migrant Daily Wage Workers: A Study in Three States

Shankar Gopalakrishnan
Trepan Singh Chauhan
Ramendra Kumar
M.S. Selvaraj

AAKAR

Conditions of Work and Political Consciousness Among Migrant Daily Wage Workers: A Study in Three States
*Shankar Gopalakrishnan, Trepan Singh Chauhan, Ramendra Kumar and M.S. Selvaraj*

First Published 2018

ISBN 978-93-5002-535-2



*Published by*
**AAKAR BOOKS**
28 E Pocket IV, Mayur Vihar Phase I,
Delhi 110 091 India
aakarbooks@gmail.com

*Laser Typeset at*
Arpit Printographers, Delhi 110 032

*Printed at*
Sapra Brothers, Noida

# Contents

# Acknowledgements

We are grateful to our research assistants Rajendra Shah, Manish Vyas, L. Priyanka and Sudita for their assistance over the course of the study.

We also owe our gratitude to our reviewers in the discussion seminar held on 6 October—Dr. K.B. Saxena, Pratyush Chandra, Sudha Bharadwaj, Surendra Pratap, Subhash Bhatnagar and members and leaders of Delhi Shramik Sanghatan—who provided valuable advice and suggestions for the study.

Finally, this study was sponsored by the Rosa Luxemburg Foundation e.V. with funds of the Federal Ministry for Economic Cooperation and Development of the Federal Republic of Germany. The Rosa Luxemburg Stiftung (RLS) is a German-based foundation working in South Asia and other parts of the world on the subjects of critical social analysis and civic education. It promotes a sovereign, socialist, secular, and democratic social order, and aims to present members of society and decision-makers with alternative approaches to such an order. Research organisations, groups working for social emancipation, and social activists are supported in their initiatives to develop models that have the potential to deliver social and economic justice.

The study would not have been possible without this generous support and the assistance of the programme manager at the foundation, Rajiv Kumar, or the South Asia Director of the foundation, Stefan Mentschel.

# Introduction

Migration is a central part of Indian society today—to the extent that Shah and Harriss-White (2011) identify it as one of the fundamental features of the country's political economy. Estimates for how many people migrate vary very widely, and there is no reliable national official data on those who do so. Estimates range from one crore to five crore people who migrate seasonally, and as for those who migrate for longer periods, there is no data at all.

However, despite the importance of migration to India's economy, and an increasing number of studies and media reports, the debate around migration in the country has remained conceptually impoverished. Outside purely academic analyses and discussions among the political left, the 'mainstream' discussion around migration looks at the issue in three primary ways.

The first is as a net "good" in terms of bringing workers out of "unproductive agriculture" (as in former Finance Minister P. Chidambaram's famous remark (Ray and Chaudhury (2008))) into other more productive occupations. This view tends to be prominent in the financial and mainstream English press, and is also mentioned in many government policy documents.

The second view sees migration as a source of crime, instability, and displacement of "locals." This takes the form of mobilisations by political parties and movements that target migrants as outsiders and treat them as a threat. Unlike the first viewpoint, this is the subject of considerable mass mobilisation, and exists in most regions of India that are areas of "destination" for migration (including places that are also sources of migrants, such as Uttarakhand).

The third view sees migration as a sign of poverty and a problem that reflects economic and policy failure, a view that is particularly common among mainstream political debates in states that are the sources of large numbers of migrants (as, again, in the case of Uttarakhand (Upadhyay (2014))).

However, all three of these viewpoints treat the migrant workers themselves as essentially invisible. On the one hand, their rights do not enter the policy or political debate at all. In recent years this information gap has been slightly reduced by a series of studies on working conditions of migrants, but these also primarily focus on large urban conglomerations and do not examine smaller cities and 'new' destinations for migrants (such as southern India). On the other hand, and perhaps more importantly, they are assumed to be largely passive actors, either "pulled" by the dynamics of capitalist growth (the mainstream view) or "pushed" out by poor conditions in their home states (the majority political view). Their own perceptions of their conditions and their political consciousness receive less attention.

In this study our focus is on addressing these two lacunae. Our study covered three field areas—one urban conglomeration where migration has already been studied to some degree, namely Delhi; and two areas where migration has received almost no academic attention, namely the city of Dehradun in Uttarakhand and the districts of Coimbatore and Nilgiris in Tamil Nadu. In all three areas we sought to examine both primary and secondary data to understand both the working conditions of migrants and the political dynamics that develop around them.

# 1

# Study Methodology and Characteristics of Our Sample

The primary data collection part of this study was conducted in the form of field surveys in the cities of Delhi and Dehradun, in Uttarakhand, and in the Nilgiris and Coimbatore districts of Tamil Nadu.

Our survey sizes were deliberately kept small—100 workers in Tamil Nadu, 98 workers in Delhi and 70 workers in Dehradun—for reasons discussed below. We did not aim for a statistically random sample, which would likely have yielded limited gains with such small sample sizes relative to a large population. Since our focus was on qualitative perceptions and experiences, we used a 'snowball' method of identifying survey participants, based on each participant's own contacts as well as the researchers' own prior contacts. Given the nature of our sample, the findings of this study should not be taken to be quantitatively or statistically precise, and our focus will be on qualitative findings.

In order to strengthen this qualitative aspect, the researchers also undertook the following steps. First, several survey areas were visited multiple times for discussions, not merely as a one time exercise in form filling. The small sample size made this feasible. In two of the three field areas (Delhi and Dehradun), the researchers are also affiliated to other autonomous organisations that engage with workers, and these experiences were also drawn upon for the study.[1] In Delhi and Dehradun, in addition, labour department officials were also interviewed.

Some key characteristics of the sample populations were as follows:

- In Dehradun and Delhi, our sample was dominated by migrant workers from Uttar Pradesh and Bihar (all of those interviewed in Dehradun and 86% of those in Delhi came from these states). In Tamil Nadu, the sample was more diverse, with workers from these states constituting 25% of the migrant workers, but others coming from Bengal, Orissa, Madhya Pradesh, Jharkhand, Assam, Andhra Pradesh and even as far afield as Nagaland (two workers).
- In age terms, our samples in Dehradun and Delhi were roughly normally distributed across age brackets, with the largest share falling between 31 years and 40 years of age (43% both field areas). Our sample in Tamil Nadu was considerably younger, with 62% being between 21 and 30 years of age and no interviewees being over 50.
- Our samples all had a majority of Hindu respondents —90% in Dehradun, 95% in Delhi and 80% in Tamil Nadu—with Muslim respondents accounting for 10% of the sample in both Dehradun and Tamil Nadu and 5% in Delhi. The only other religious community represented was Christians, which accounted for 10%

1. In the discussion below, conclusions that have been drawn on the basis of prior experience rather than the research for this study are referred to as such.

of the sample in Tamil Nadu (but were not part of the sample in the other survey areas).

- Dalit respondents formed the largest share of those interviewed in each survey area—70% in Delhi and 43% in Tamil Nadu.[2] The remainder of those interviewed belonged to Other Backward Caste communities, except in Tamil Nadu, where 30% of those interviewed were from the Scheduled Tribes. A very small population of those interviewed were from forward or general castes, accounting for 2% in the Delhi sample.
- The majority of those we interviewed were in daily wage construction jobs—accounting for 85% of those interviewed in Delhi, all of those interviewed in Dehradun and 70% of those interviewed in Tamil Nadu. Within the construction sector, the largest share—70% of the total sample in Dehradun, 74% in Delhi, and 80% in Tamil Nadu—were either masons or unskilled workers who worked alongside masons. The remainder of interviewees worked in small shops or in other daily wage and informal sector occupations.
- Most of our sample had low education levels. In Delhi, 40% of those interviewed had no education, another 30% had only a primary education, and all except one worker had not studied past the tenth standard. The distribution in Dehradun was similar, with the exception of 5% of workers who had completed to more than 10th standard (and one worker who had completed his graduation). In Tamil

2. Unfortunately, there were issues with data collection on this point in Dehradun.

Nadu, the sample had a higher overall educational level, with 62% having completed up to the 10th standard level and 4% having completed graduation.

- In Delhi and Dehradun, most of our sample was married (93% and 88% respectively) and a large proportion lived with their families (87% and 82% respectively). In Tamil Nadu, in contrast, only 22% were married and only 16% lived with their families.

One key point that requires further explanation is the gender balance in our samples, which were overwhelmingly male (90% of those interviewed in Delhi, 95% of those interviewed in Dehradun and 77% in Tamil Nadu). This gender imbalance was a reflection of two facts. First, we were interviewing workers at the sites of destination, where the migrant workforce in daily wage work is indeed majority male (see discussion in next section); and second, our survey methodology, which focused on "snowball" methods of identifying workers through people they knew, and which hence skewed the sample further towards men. The findings of this study are hence more representative of the experiences of *male* migrant workers.[3]

Though we are cautious about drawing any conclusions about overall characteristics in the absence of rigorous random sampling in our surveys, we do feel that these sample populations are broadly representative of some trends among informal sector migrant workers. The caste, religious and work profiles of our sample broadly accord with both prior reports as well as the researchers' own

3. Some explorations of the experience of migrant women workers can be found in Chauhan and Gopalakrishnan (2014), by two of the present researchers, and in Gopalakrishnan, Chauhan, and Kumar (2014).

experiences. While the construction sector may seem overrepresented, construction is a major source of employment for migrant workers (a point also referred to in most of the existing literature); see, for instance, the discussions in Sharma and Khandewal (2014) and Srivastava and Sasikumar (2003)). Moreover, construction is particularly important for the role it plays in one part of the migration cycle, as we discuss in the next section.

The sample for Tamil Nadu is an outlier in some respects, but in these respects it also seems to reflect certain features specific to inter-state migration into the informal sector in Tamil Nadu. Unlike Delhi and Uttarakhand, mass migration from north Indian states into Tamil Nadu is a relatively more recent phenomenon. While we are not aware of any official studies on this issue, anecdotal evidence confirms that such migration has greatly increased over the preceding two decades, and a recent survey by the government established that there are now over a million migrant workers in the state (Philip 2016). The fact that such a large number of people have moved recently affects both the politicisation and the nature of the migrant community, a point that we will return to in the next section.

In addition to the above, the study relies on secondary data, including prior studies, official data and media reports.

# 2

# Background: Understanding the Dynamics of Working Class Migration in India

As noted above, there is little rigorous official data on the number of working class people who migrate in India. The Census primarily seeks to capture long-term migration. NSSO surveys have attempted to measure "short-term" migration, but the figures they report are well below those estimated by other researchers (Sharma and Khandewal 2014; Agrawal and Chandrasekhar 2015). One estimate by the latter places seasonal migration at 100 million people a year (Deshingkar and Start 2003).

Migration in daily wage and casual labour operates through a number of different mechanisms. While our focus in this study has been on conditions at the sites of destination for migrants, we can also briefly examine the process of migration itself, on which both prior studies and our survey reveal some key factors.

The reasons for migration are widespread and varied. At a general level, some of the factors often named as responsible for migration are the following:

- *The agrarian crisis and the collapse of earnings from agriculture*: The unremunerative nature of agriculture —in particular, following the agrarian crisis over the last two decades and the accompanying collapse of much of the rural economy—is perhaps the most common and fundamental cause for migration in much of the country. In our study, this was reflected by the fact that the majority of our respondents in all three survey sites who responded to questions about their employment prior to migration—78% in Dehradun, 92% in Tamil Nadu and 82% in Delhi—reported that they had been either cultivators or agricultural labourers prior to migration. Many had also had land. All our respondents in Dehradun reported owning more than half an acre in their home villages (a surprising 18% reported owning more than five acres, though this appears to have partly reflected the income from migration). 62% of those in Tamil Nadu had had land, of which three quarters owned between half an acre and an acre. In Delhi the proportion was lower—37% reported owning land—but a third of these owned five acres or more. In the best indicator of the role of the agricultural crisis in migration, in Dehradun respondents were also asked how many of them had been both cultivators and farm workers prior to migrating, and 77% of those who responded to the question about prior employment chose this option—demonstrating a prior dependence on wage labour because of the lack of agricultural income.

- *Middle class positions leading to particular forms of migration*: It has also been postulated that the poorest and the most marginalised in fact do not manage to undertake the kind of migration we discuss here, where small groups of workers leave, often on their own resources, to do work elsewhere. This requires a certain minimum level of assets before it becomes a viable option (tickets need to be purchased, assets need to be bought in the area of destination, there needs to be enough money to ensure that those who stay behind can survive until the migrant can send money, and so on). Poorer communities may migrate shorter distances, or do so over longer distances under relations of debt bondage. Richer and more powerful communities may migrate for specific forms of work (security guards, for instance[4]). This middle position does appear to be reflected in our survey. The land ownership statistics above are one indicator. Further, 19% of those interviewed in Delhi and 10% of those interviewed in Dehradun reported earning more than Rs. 5,000 a month from agricultural activities in their home areas (the proportion for Tamil Nadu was considerably lower —76% reported being able to earn between Rs. 1,000 and 2,000 a month, and only 4% reported earnings over Rs. 3,000, with none earning more than Rs. 4,000; we return to this point below).

- *Changing labour relations in rural areas*: A final point that has been noted by many prior scholars is the changing structure of labour relations in rural areas over the past several decades. In particular, the decline of caste-based "personal" labour relations in favour of long-term contracts; changes from patronage and payment in kind to cash-based, contractual relationships; the decline in the ability of employers to use physical force to bind workers to

4. We are indebted to Pratyush Chandra, one of our peer reviewers, for raising this point.

> work; and other such changes have made it both possible and necessary for more people to migrate. These issues do not really fall within our scope here; they are discussed in more depth in other sources, such as Rao (1999) and Gopalakrishnan and Sreenivasa (2009).

All these factors affect both the economic position of migrants and their political responses to their living situations. We will return to this question in the discussion on the political consciousness that accompanies migration below.

**Flows of Migration**

Discussions on migrant daily wage workers often discuss "migrants" as if all such workers operate under the same conditions or work constraints. Drawing on our prior experience, we have found that this impression can be misleading.

For instance, even among daily wage and construction workers in the kind of urban and semi-urban areas that we examined—in other words, among one subset of poor migrant workers—we can broadly distinguish a four stage transition in working situations that many workers undergo:

*Stage 1*: Individual men migrate out of their home area, often through contacts with friends, relatives, or caste members from the same original village. These men may shift from location to location as well, a point reflected in our survey results, where 41% of those interviewed in Tamil Nadu, 33% in Dehradun and 30% in Delhi indicated that they had initially migrated elsewhere.

At this stage, workers often stay several to a rented room, squeezing in with other single men and sharing cooking among themselves. Agricultural harvests and retail trade may offer employment to workers at this stage, but in urban and semi-urban environments the most common form of employment is likely to be daily wage work in the construction sector (which also reflects the rapid growth of real estate and construction in cities). Such workers are often those who go to the *mazdoor chowks*—the roadside sites where workers gather in the mornings—to seek work.

A subset of these people are those who are specifically brought in to construction sites by larger contractors. Such people usually stay at the work site, however, and often move on to new sites afterwards. As a result, they are both extremely difficult to organise and difficult to survey.

*Stage* 2: If a worker remains in a single site for a long enough period and finds enough work, they may undergo a shift in both accommodation and class status. In the construction sector, workers may learn enough of the trade to shift out of the position of being an unskilled *mazdoor* (to use the Hindi term) to become a mason (*mistri*) or, if they are literate, potentially a plumber or a carpenter. This will increase their income and security, and most such workers stop going to the chowks for work. They may then also move to slightly better accommodation, perhaps less crowded.

*Stage* 3: If they succeed in moving to stage 2, workers often consider bringing their wives and children to their site of work. Many workers choose to never do so (such as one participant in our survey in Dehradun, whose wife had a small-scale job in an anganwadi in Bihar and who had no interest in migrating to Dehradun), but those who do will then shift into independent rented accommodation, typically with one or two rooms.

*Stage* 4: After they feel secure in employment and financial terms in their new location, workers may choose to build their own homes in their site of work. As we discuss in the section on discrimination below, these houses are almost always constructed on government land, but that does not mean the land is "encroached." It is more often "purchased" from an earlier occupier, a purchase that is usually recorded in a sale deed, and the new house built by the worker using their savings or other assets. Workers who reach this stage may then stay in the area for decades, gradually reducing their visits to their areas of origin and selling off assets there. Children study in the new area and may have little contact with the area of origin. Referring to workers who reach stage 4 as "migrants" may seem an odd formulation, but for reasons discussed below, in several respects they continue very much to be "migrants"—and this identity shapes their role in other ways.

The transition from stage 1 to stage 4 takes a wildly varying amount of time and is by no means inevitable. Many workers will not transition out of stage 2 for many years, and some workers who do may be pushed back to stage 2 if they are hit by a personal disaster or health emergency that ends up forcing them to send their family back to the area of origin.

Moreover, the site of destination affects how easy it is to transition through these stages. One of the distinct features of our Tamil Nadu survey sample is that migrants from non-Tamil speaking states—those referred to generically as "north Indians" by both media and officials in Tamil Nadu—are likely to find it extremely difficult to ever make it to stage 3, since language issues make this much harder. Furthermore, overt discrimination is both easier and far more extreme in such a context. We discuss these issues further in the section on discrimination below.

Finally, it should also be noted that, like many informal sector workers, migrant workers often do not stick to form of work. Workers in the first stage, and sometimes in the second stage, may keep shifting types of work as they seek better incomes. For instance, workers in our survey reported that they might shift between daily wage construction work, work as a vegetable vendor or newspaper delivery person, and, in one case, even setting up a small snack stand for a period. Workers also often engage in multiple forms of work —for instance, doing construction work when it is available, loading goods in the mandi when it is not, and so on. This shifting of jobs tends to reduce in workers who reach the third or the fourth stage, as reaching that point usually means they have settled into one line of work and developed sufficient contacts to ensure they have enough work to feel reasonably secure.

All these transitions have impacts on workers' conditions, status and consciousness, and we will return to this point in the discussions on discrimination and political consciousness below.

# 3

# Conditions of Life and Work

Our survey examined working conditions among migrant informal sector workers, beginning with basic questions of wages and livelihoods. Our findings were both disturbing and unsurprising.

## Wages

Wages were, as expected, extremely low in all three sites. In Dehradun and Tamil Nadu the largest proportion of those interviewed had estimated monthly incomes that fell within the brackets of Rs. 5,000-Rs. 7,000 (37% in Dehradun and 49% in Tamil Nadu), while the reported incomes were slightly higher in Delhi (48% reported incomes between Rs. 7,000-Rs. 10,000 per month). There were outliers on both sides in Delhi and Dehradun, while five people reported an income higher than Rs. 10,000 in Tamil Nadu.

It should be noted that as per minimum wage regulations that are in force at present, an unskilled worker in the construction sector who works for 25 days in a month should receive Rs. 8,075 in Tamil Nadu, Rs. 3,750 in Uttarakhand and Rs. 12,825 in Delhi respectively. Out of our sample, 84% of those in Delhi and 49% of those in Tamil Nadu are earning well below the minimum wage. Uttarakhand's extremely low minimum wages meant that only 8% of our sample reported earning less than the minimum wage. But this reflects the weakness of Uttarakhand's minimum wage legislation, not any better situation for workers.

This becomes apparent when we examine expenses. In almost all cases in all three locations, the reported monthly expenses almost equalled, or exceeded, the workers' earnings. Sending money home—a standard reason for migration—was often a sporadic activity based on momentary surpluses. We did not seek to evaluate levels of debt in our survey, but it was very commonly reported by our discussants.

## Working Conditions and Labour Rights

Labour law, as it would apply to migrant workers in the informal sector, is not limited to one statute, but instead constitutes a kind of broad set of principles that are enunciated in multiple statutes—as well as a vacuum of legal protection for most situations in which workers find themselves (for which see below). The full legal regime that applies to these workers is a highly complex subject, with multiple and often contradictory court rulings, and we will not discuss it in detail here. Our primary focus is on the *political* and *institutional* aspects of law enforcement when it comes to the labour rights of workers.

The first statute that is often noted in regard to migrant workers is the Inter-State Migrant Workers' (Regulation of Employment and Conditions of Service) Act, 1979, which is essentially India's only national law explicitly intended to cover migrant workers. One might expect that—being inter-state migrants—workers like those in our sample would be automatically covered by this law, but in practice the ISMW Act excludes most of the workers in the informal sector because it only applies to workers hired by a contractor in one state for work in *another* state. In our sample, and in our field observations, the majority of migrant workers do not migrate on the basis of explicit contracts from out of state contractors. They are more likely to come on the basis of family relationships or friends, though they may obtain work through contractors after arriving. By including a condition like this, the government has thus effectively made the ISMW Act irrelevant to all except a small handful of large contracting companies that hire across states.[5]

However, the ISMW Act reiterates certain basic principles of law that are also contained in other statutes—notably the Contract Labour (Regulation and Abolition) Act, 1971, and the Building and Other Construction Workers (Regulation of Employment and Conditions of Service) Act, 1996, both of which would apply to a significant proportion of the workers in our sample for much of the time. Some of the basic rights provided for in these laws include the following:

- The "principal employer"—or the person or agency for whose benefit the work is done—is ultimately liable for the workers' wages and working conditions, and for maintenance of records. If the workers are hired by a contractor who fails to meet these requirements, the employer must do so. Working hours are limited to a 48 hour work week.[6]
- Wages have to be paid within a fixed maximum time period (one week after completion of work in the case of the Building Workers' Act). Under the Minimum Wages Act, minimum wages must be paid.

5. See Sharma and Khandewal (2014) for a similar discussion on this law.
6. It should be noted that the provisions relating to the principal employer are now under threat in the proposed "wage code" of the current NDA government.

- Certain minimum facilities, including canteens, restrooms, creches, safety gear, etc. have to be provided in work sites to which these laws apply.

In practice, as our survey revealed and as any casual observer would note, very few of these legal requirements are met. The basic facilities requirement is, to put it politely, a joke. Practically no work site provides all these facilities, and all but the largest do not provide any of them.

Perhaps the best reflection of this failure is health difficulties among migrant workers, which were widely reported in our sample. In Tamil Nadu, 87% of those surveyed said they experienced health problems; in Dehradun 75% said so; and in Delhi 94% said the same. The most commonly cited health issues were back and leg pain and exhaustion-related illnesses, such as headaches and fevers. Physical injury was also commonly reported by our workers—either as having occurred to themselves or to others—ranging from minor scratches and bruises up to fractures, amputations and death. Notwithstanding the provisions of the Workers' Compensation Act and these laws, none of our participants in Delhi and Dehradun and only 10% of our sample in Tamil Nadu reported receiving any assistance with such injuries or health conditions at all. Anecdotally, we were told of incidents where contractors or employers had provided cash payments to workers who were injured, but these were typically one time payoffs with no contribution to the workers' ongoing medical expenses (in the next section we discuss welfare schemes that are ostensibly meant to address these gaps).

Similarly, legal provisions regarding wage payments are essentially never enforced. While we did not include an explicit question on this in our survey, one of the most commonly reported problems for migrant workers was non-payment or underpayment of wages. Since wages are typically paid in a lump sum at the end of a period of work, or in sums spread over the period of work, the contractor or employer will often simply fail to pay an instalment, or pay part of it and ask for time to pay the rest. Under both the Contract Labour (Regulation and Abolition) Act and/or the Building Workers Act, delaying payment beyond the statutory time period is an offence and ensuring payment is the responsibility of the principal employer, if a contractor fails to do so. But neither workers nor, in our experience, employers are aware of these laws. Indeed, even Labour Department officials are unaware of them. For instance, in one case that the Dehradun-based researchers are aware of, the following occurred.[7]

A migrant worker from Bihar was denied payment by his employer after a painting job when his employer, a factory owner, paid only part of his wages. The worker approached labour department officials and was told to produce written proof that he had worked at this site. Since the only written proof he had was a slip of paper on which he had tracked his payments, he was told nothing would be done. When he approached his union, the union contacted the employer and was told that the employer was "unsatisfied" with the work and that no further payment would be made. The union subsequently took up the matter with the Labour Department and submitted a written representation pointing out that—as the Building Workers' Act happened to apply to this case—the responsibility for

7. Disclosure: researchers Shankar Gopalakrishnan and Trepan Singh Chauhan were involved in representing the worker in this case as part of their work as organisers with the Uttarakhand Nav Nirman Mazdoor Sangh.

maintaining records of payment and employment was on the employer, not the worker, and that in the absence of such records the workers' viewpoint should prevail. Partly as a result of this legal argument and partly because the union was involved, the labour officials relented and summoned the employer, who eventually paid the worker.

In sum, it would be fair to say that, for migrant workers in the informal sector, labour law provisions might as well not exist. In this sense, of course, migrants only replicate the experience of the majority of informal sector workers though with an additional layer of discrimination. This fundamental experience is rooted in the following essential features of India's labour law regime:

- *Limits on applicability*: Most of India's main labour laws include numerical limits on the minimum number of workers at a worksite before they become applicable. In the case of the Building Workers' Act, this is 10 workers, and in the case of the Contract Labour Act the limit is 20 workers. Since the majority of construction and informal sector worksites fall under these limits, this automatically means that most workers, most of the time, have no labour law protection at all.
- *Restrictions on the filing of complaints*: As if this were not enough, all of India's labour laws, with rare exceptions, provide that violations of their provisions will be a criminal offence—and then effectively nullify this provision by making it impossible for the affected worker to directly file a criminal complaint. Thus, under the Minimum Wages Act or the Contract Labour Act, only the Labour Inspector can file a police complaint. The Building Workers' Act slightly liberalised this provision by allowing a registered

trade union of construction workers to also do so. The result of these restrictions is that the entire structure of these laws effectively becomes a dead letter, since they disempower the people most affected by their violations.

- *Burden of proof*: While these laws do, implicitly, place the burden of proof on the employer, the combination of the above provisions means that the actual burden of proof is on the worker. A worker facing a violation of their rights must first establish that the law applies to them and then convince a labour official (or a union official, if a union exists) that their rights have been violated. All of this has to happen *before* the complaint receives any formal recognition at all.

In effect this means that for the majority of informal sector workers, for most of the time, there is no legal regime that protects any of their rights. This problem is not limited to migrant workers, of course. But it affects them with particular severity because it is then compounded by the reality of discrimination, which we return to below.

In their remarks during our interviews, labour department officials themselves seemed to treat the issue as if labour laws and labour rights were irrelevant. In Delhi and Dehradun, labour officials informed us that they had no ability or interest in implementing the ISMW Act (indeed, in a 2011 written response, the Uttarakhand Labour Department had stated that it had not registered any workers under that Act). Under the Building Workers' Act, as well, they were neither aware of nor interested in enforcing the labour rights provisions of the law. In all three survey sites, it was apparent that the law's extensive safety requirements, which run into tens of pages, were being completely ignored by officials.

Instead, for labour officials, the only rights of migrant workers that were seen as relevant were their right to receive welfare entitlements, particularly under the schemes provided for in the Building Workers' Act. The Delhi officials also mentioned a Bihar government scheme of compensating the kin of migrant workers who die, a scheme about which the Dehradun officials appear to be unaware. In Tamil Nadu, even this level of awareness was not present, and the workers we interviewed had never seen nor heard of the Labour Department or its role—either as enforcer of the law or as provider of welfare.

**Access to Welfare Entitlements**

Given that government agencies see migrant workers purely through the prism of welfare schemes, are these, at least, being implemented? The answer, as one might expect, is no.

Under the law, migrant workers (and indeed all poor citizens) broadly have access to three types of entitlements:

- Access to the public distribution system (the 'ration' system) for food and basic supplies.
- Public health care, including both the government hospital system and health insurance schemes such as the Rashtriya Swasth Bima Yojana.
- Sector-specific welfare benefits, such as those that flow from registration under the Building Workers' Act.

On all these fronts, our survey showed, migrant workers suffer severe problems in accessing their rights. We discuss each of these separately below.

It first bears mentioning, however, that the one form of government document that practically all of our sample (except in Tamil Nadu) possessed was Aadhaar cards. All those interviewed in Dehradun, all except one in Delhi, and 74% of those interviewed in Tamil Nadu had Aadhaar cards. In the case of Tamil Nadu these had all been obtained in their home areas, while in the other two field areas roughly 75% of those interviewed had obtained these cards in their current location. This is a testimony to the success of the central government's drive to compulsorily register people for Aadhaar, and, in the process, to collect their biometric details and other information in its databases. In itself, however, the Aadhaar card offers no access to any particular entitlement.

### *The Public Distribution System*

Access to the PDS is restricted to those who possess a ration card for the area in which they live. But in all our samples, the majority of those interviewed did not meet this condition and hence did not have access to the local ration system. This was because they either did not have ration cards (47% Delhi and 30% in Dehradun) or did not have ration cards for the area where they are now working (15% of those who had ration cards in Dehradun and 29% in Delhi). In net, this meant that 75% of those interviewed in Delhi, 40% of those interviewed in Dehradun and all of those we interviewed in Tamil Nadu did not have local ration cards (in Tamil Nadu those interviewed were only asked if they had a local ration card, and not if they had one in their home area).

This becomes a particularly severe problem for migrant workers who are living without their families. Workers who are alone have no time to purchase supplies in the day, and must do so in the evening (obviously, the lack of refrigerators in most such households means that buying vegetables, in the warm season, has to be done daily or at most every two to three days). Local traders, being aware of this pattern, hike their prices accordingly at this time. Over time this adds up to a considerable additional expense for these workers.

Further, aside from this direct financial impact, lack of local ration cards effectively bars workers from accessing many of the most important welfare schemes of central and state governments (such as their entitlements under the Food Security Act, subsidised kerosene, and multiple other schemes that 'welfare-friendly' governments like Tamil Nadu run through the ration shops).

### *Health Schemes*

Migrant workers, like all of India's poor, find it difficult to rely on the catastrophically underfunded public health care system in the case of health emergencies. Since securing effective and swift care is often impossible, they then turn to private practitioners.

In the name of helping workers in such a situation, both central and state governments operate a number of health insurance schemes for those under the poverty line and certain categories of workers. The most widespread of these is the Rashtriya Swasth Bima Yojana, under which workers are issued with a "health smartcard" that covers up to Rs. 30,000 per year in costs related to any illness that leads to hospital admission. Several types of informal workers are meant to be automatically covered by the RSBY—for instance, under guidelines issued in March 2013, registered construction workers should receive cards under RSBY without requiring action on their part and without requiring them to pay the normal premium.[8] Similarly, the scheme is meant to also cover all domestic workers and street vendors,

8. Central Government, Ministry of Health and Family Welfare, "Guidelines for Extension of the RSBY To Building and Other Construction Workers", dated March 4, 2013.

to mention some other forms of work in which migrant informal sector workers are likely to engage in at some point in their working life. Meanwhile, most states run their own insurance schemes that provide similar entitlements, such as the Mukhyamantri Swasth Bima Yojana in Uttarakhand.

Considering that health care emergencies are the single biggest reason that Indians are pushed into poverty and destitution, access to health care welfare schemes can be critical to maintaining one's financial security. But, as we saw above, the vast majority of our survey participants reported receiving no assistance with health care expenses at all. In discussions, barring a handful of people, the workers confirmed that they had not received smart cards or been registered under the RSBY, and those who had received such cards (such as in Dehradun) were frequently denied their entitlements when they sought to obtain them for hospitalisation expenses. Hospitals refused to accept the cards or claimed that they were not aware of any such scheme, and workers were forced to pay for their costs out of pocket.

### *Registration Under the Building and Other Construction Workers' Act*

The majority of our sample, as we saw, are people who characterise themselves as construction workers at present. It is also important to note that, in the process of shifting of work forms that we noted in the section above on migration flows, a large proportion of informal sector male migrant workers—perhaps the majority—will engage in construction work at some point or on a frequent basis, even if it is not their main form of labour.

This means that registration under the Building Workers' Act, and access to the welfare entitlements under the schemes that operate under it, is a crucial form of welfare provision for a large number of migrant informal sector workers. These schemes vary from state to state, but typically involve some kind of scholarship assistance for the education of children, grants for major expenses like funerals and marriages, and grants for provision of basic equipment like toolkits (or, in the case of Dehradun, cycles and solar lanterns). Hence we specifically explored the extent to which workers in our sample were able to obtain their entitlements under this law.

The answers varied widely by site. In both Delhi and Dehradun, our sample included large numbers of people affiliated to unions[9] that have specifically sought registration of their members, and hence our results were skewed upwards on this question—63% of our sample in Delhi and 78% in Dehradun reported that they were registered. But none of our participants in Tamil Nadu reported being registered, though, as noted, 80% of those interviewed were currently working in construction-related work.

This is consistent with the findings of other studies, which have shown that registration under this Act remains non-existent until there is mass mobilisation around it. In Uttarakhand, for instance, a written RTI reply received in November 2011 revealed that only 157 workers had been registered under this law in all of Garhwal mandal, and no welfare benefits had been provided to any worker. Following prolonged mobilisation by the union of daily wage workers, total registration in the state crossed one lakh in 2016. This is even more true of receiving entitlements under this Act.

9. Disclosure: researchers Ramendra Kumar, Trepan Singh Chauhan and Shankar Gopalakrishnan are associated with these unions.

No one in Tamil Nadu had received any entitlements, which is hardly surprising considering that that they were not registered. In Dehradun, the process of distribution of entitlements began in earnest only in 2016. Prior to this there had been almost no distribution, and in 2011, as said above, the government's written response stated that no entitlements had been distributed.

### Unionisation

As we noted above, one of the artifacts of our survey methodology was that our samples in Dehradun and Delhi both included large numbers of workers affiliated to unions (75% and 62% respectively). No one in Tamil Nadu was affiliated to any union. The fact that this distinction was a survey artifact makes it difficult to use this for comparative purposes, since any comparison seeking to examine the effects of unionisation would have to include a control group in both cities that was not affiliated to or aware of the unions at all (as those in Tamil Nadu were). Further, such an attempt to measure the success of unionisation as such would involve a conflict of interest for the researchers, since in both Dehradun and Delhi they are also affiliated to the said unions.

Hence, while our study design does not permit us to examine the effects of unionisation *per se*, we can look at some of the dynamics that this unionisation process has produced in each area, and the manner in which these were reflected in our survey results.

One distinction that is apparent in our survey results, and by comparison with past data in both Delhi and Dehradun, shows that unions have had a marked impact on the implementation of welfare schemes (as noted in the previous section). However, given the apparent commonalities between the three study sites, it is also clear that union organisation has not yet been able to secure wages, working conditions, or (as discussed in the next section) related issues like housing. This reflects what one might call the uneven political and institutional landscape on which unionisation occurs—a key challenge in efforts to change working conditions. We return to this discussion in the last section, on ways forward.

# 4

# Discrimination

Perhaps unsurprisingly, many of our sample respondents reported feeling discriminated against. These figures were lowest in Dehradun, ranging from 10-15% on various discrimination-related questions—for reasons that will be discussed further below. In Delhi, 74% of those interviewed reported experiencing discrimination, while in Tamil Nadu 79% did so (when asked in general; when asked about discrimination from the police, this rose to 90%). This discrimination could be broadly broken down into the following types.

## Discrimination in Housing

Difficulty in obtaining housing was the most widely reported problem faced by the workers in our sample. 71%, 41% and 30% of those interviewed in Tamil Nadu, Dehradun and Delhi respectively answered "yes" when asked if they had difficulty obtaining housing.

The forms of discrimination that were reported included a reluctance on the part of landlords to rent places to stay to workers, and the reluctance of neighbours and other residents to permit migrant workers to stay in their area. This was particularly common in Tamil Nadu, where 39% and 32% of our sample, respectively, reported these forms of discrimination. A third form of discrimination was facing demands for extra rent as compared to 'locals.' The latter was more common than one might expect; fully 86% of those interviewed in Tamil Nadu reported experiencing this, and having to pay up to Rs. 500 extra for their residence. Similarly, 44% of those interviewed in Delhi said that they had to pay extra, though they reported a much higher discrepancy in terms of rent, with the majority saying they needed to pay around Rs. 1,000 extra a month. 21% of workers in Dehradun also reported facing higher rents.

Moreover, since such discrimination tends to ghettoise migrant workers into particular slums and neighbourhoods, the actual discrimination they experience can be far more severe than these figures indicate. This was indicated by our findings regarding the conditions under which most of these workers live.

In Delhi, fully 84% of those interviewed stayed in a residence consisting of only one room, while only 3% had residences that had more than two rooms. Of those who stayed in one room, 64% had four or more people staying in that room, with 13% reporting that seven or more people were staying in their room. In Dehradun, 63% reported that they were staying in a residence with only one room, and 80% of those who reported staying in one room reported that four or more people were staying in it (11% said that seven or more were staying in their single room). In Tamil Nadu, none of the workers stayed in any residence with more than two rooms, while 62% stayed in a residence with only one room, and while no one reported that more than four people lived in their accommodation, 62% reported that four did so.

These figures are, of course, just the tip of the iceberg. Urban and semi-urban slums of the kind where migrant workers stay are extraordinarily poorly served by basic infrastructure, lacking piped water, sewage connections, cleaning services or proper streets. While toilets are considerably more common than is often realised by non slum-dwellers, living conditions are very unsanitary as a result of the lack of public garbage collection. For single migrant workers in the "first stage" of migration discussed above, the standard accommodation is to have anywhere from three to ten men sharing a small brick room with a tin roof, with a kerosene stove in a corner for cooking (in the case of Tamil Nadu, migrant workers used large shared pots to cook rice). Fans are a rarity in such rooms, which become unbearably hot in the summer. Moreover, the average rents of such accommodations are considerably higher than they are in other parts of the city. In Dehradun, it is not unusual for a worker staying in a shared room of this kind to be paying Rs. 600 or even Rs. 700 a month. Multiplied by eight men, this adds up to an amount sufficient to rent a one or two bedroom flat (with piped water and electricity) in the cheaper parts of the city.

But, of course, such migrant workers would never be allowed to rent a flat. It might be objected that these living conditions apply to all poor workers and informal sector workers, but even within these classes, there is a marked difference in the conditions experienced by migrants and by others. For instance, domestic and daily wage workers of Uttarakhandi background in Dehradun, or Tamils in Tamil Nadu, are able to rent small accommodations in "colonies" and neighbourhoods, while migrants were rarely able to escape slums.

### Discrimination by the Police

The second form of discrimination that we asked about was discrimination by the police. This was reported by 90% of those interviewed in Tamil Nadu, 26% in Delhi and 14% in Dehradun.

Discrimination from the police was reported in two primary forms. The first was arbitrary violence. 21% of those interviewed in Tamil Nadu who reported discrimination from the police, and one third of those who did so in Dehradun, said that this took the form of beatings. Both these figures are likely to be underestimates, as workers often did not report police violence as "discrimination" as such. For instance, in Dehradun, until the mobilisation referred to earlier, police lathi charges on workers standing on roadsides for work in the morning were a near weekly affair.

The second form of discrimination was the registration of false cases against migrant workers. There was a general perception, across all three sites, that unsolved thefts, burglaries or murders would be pinned on migrant workers by the police. This was extremely common in Tamil Nadu, where 71% of our sample reported that they had faced scapegoating like this.

In themselves, such false cases against poor and working class people are not unusual, but they are particularly difficult for migrant workers to fight, as they lack the local connections that are vital in handling the police—such as access to a lawyer or friendly relations with other police officials. When lawyers are approached, they frequently charge exorbitant amounts; one worker in Dehradun who was detained under Section 151 of the Criminal Procedure Code, which should result in automatic release upon signing of a personal bond, paid Rs. 8,000 to a lawyer under the false belief that he needed to obtain "bail."

There is a third form of discrimination by the police that is difficult to measure, and that is their neglect in protecting the rights of workers. In cases of non-payment of wages or violence by employers, workers were often reluctant to approach the police for assistance, as they feared that the police would accept bribes from the opposite party and do nothing—or, worse, beat up the worker.

**Discrimination by Other Arms of the Government**

Other forms of discrimination were also reported. Closely related to the housing issue was the attitude of municipal corporations and the revenue department, which views migrants as "encroachers" on public lands. Indeed, urban and land use planning in India essentially never takes into account the needs of migrant workers, who form the most "invisible" part of the informal sector in policy terms (at most, municipalities or labour officials may provide a few night shelters, or "rann baseras"; the Delhi Labour Department runs several of these in the city). Everything from the places where migrant workers live, to the public facilities they use, to the places where they stand for work, are ignored by state land use planning agencies.[10]

As a result, periodic evictions of slums have been both brutal and common in Delhi and Tamil Nadu (though far from unknown, they have been proportionately less common in Dehradun). Eviction is not simply a matter of people losing a place to stay, which would be devastating enough. Those in stage four of migration, who may own their houses, face the loss of what may be their largest asset by far, and hence the destruction of a lifetime's worth of savings. Tenants are not immune, as they often lose property and documents when evictions take place. Repeated evictions are one of the most devastating blows to workers in general and migrant workers in particular.

Finally, there is the approach of the Labour Department, which we discussed in the preceding section on labour

10. See Gopalakrishnan and Chauhan (2014) for a discussion of one example of this.

rights. None of the workers we interviewed felt that the Labour Department sought to represent their interests, and as we saw above, labour officials seem to feel that there is in fact no need to do so. Once again, this is nothing unusual as far as the working class in general is concerned. Labour departments across India are understaffed, apathetic, undercut by legal and policy changes, and generally utter failures as far as the rights of workers are concerned. But in the case of migrant workers, these factors join together with discrimination and isolation in a perfect storm of factors that essentially deprive these workers of all legal rights.

**Forms and Extremes of Discrimination**

There are clear distinctions in the forms and level of discrimination that we observed. As the data above shows, our sample in Tamil Nadu experienced by far the most overt and severe forms of discrimination, while those in Dehradun experienced, comparatively, the least. This reflects the factors discussed in the section on migration flows. Lacking knowledge of the local language, migrants in Tamil Nadu are essentially cut off entirely from local society, and are easy targets for both state agencies and chauvinist politicians (the latter are discussed further in the next section). As a result, they tend to remain in the first or second stage of migration; in our survey, 80% of those interviewed said they planned to return to their home areas.

In contrast, in Dehradun, our sample consisted of a much more settled population—only 10% of those interviewed expressed any desire to return to their home areas, while 27% had been out of their home areas so long that they preferred to identify themselves as "from Dehradun" as their first response (though they were migrants in the sense that they were neither Uttarakhandi nor had been born there).

Many of these people were also in the fourth stage of migration, with children in school in Dehradun and only returning to their areas of origin for a few days in a year. To clarify, this was not necessarily a reflection of the migrant population in general, but only of the characteristics of those in our sample.

But this great difference in our sample population only serves to highlight one stark reality of migration—how much even settled, largely Hindi-speaking migrants, in a Hindi speaking state, *continue* to face forms of oppression and violence similar to what would appear to be their much more disadvantaged counterparts in Tamil Nadu. We noted above how many problems are shared across our three samples, notwithstanding how *different* these groups of workers actually are. This highlights a basic and often unnoticed reality of migration in India—migrants in the informal sector are never accepted as full residents of their areas of work and never treated as equal citizens, even after decades, in contrast to professional migrants. This contributes to the political environment that develops around them, as discussed in the next section.

# 5

# Political Dynamics Around Migration

Migration is a central political issue across India, and we can broadly refer to three primary ways in which the issue is politicised (as discussed in the introduction). The first of these is "nativist" political mobilisation against migrants. The second is the political organisation of migrants themselves, which is considerably rarer than the first. The third is political mobilisation in states of origin, where political leaders or organisations claim that they will take steps to stop migration from being necessary. Since our focus is on the politics of sites of destination, we focus on the first two forms here.

## Mobilisation Against Migrants

All three states that we covered have witnessed political mobilisation against inter-state migrant workers, and as in all such mobilisations, it is daily wage and informal sector workers who are the first targets.

In Tamil Nadu, beatings, lynchings of migrant workers, and police killings (in the form of "encounters") of inter-state migrant workers have all occurred (Dutta 2012; Warrier 2012). In 2012, following a bank robbery, the state government also initiated an exercise of "verifying" all "north Indian" workers and students in the state, and conducted a state-wide census of these workers. Political leaders routinely refer to "North Indians" as the source of rising crime. The vast majority of trade unions and political parties, including those of the Left, have failed to respond to the atrocities and attacks on migrant workers that have occurred. All of this contributes greatly to the atmosphere of harassment and fear that we noted above, including difficulty in finding housing, higher costs and false police cases. The combination of these incidents and the data we have discussed above indicate that Tamil Nadu is extremely hostile to the rights of migrant workers at present.

In Uttarakhand, anti-migrant hostility is considerably less open than in Tamil Nadu, and in the present environment it is rare to find openly anti-migrant statements from politicians or senior officials. One reason for this is the fact that both the major political parties in Uttarakhand (the Congress and the BJP) are "national" parties and cannot openly speak against those from outside the state, while the regional party—the Uttarakhand Kranti Dal—is extremely weak. However, undercurrents of prejudice are very strong in the state, and themes of "throwing out" migrants were voiced both during and after the Uttarakhand movement. In the experience of the researchers, prior to the growth of the union mobilisation in Dehradun, lower officials were openly anti-migrant and referred to migrant daily wage workers as drunkards, thieves and criminals.[11] They also asked why the Uttarakhand government should be responsible for their welfare or rights, since that was the "business of the Bihar and UP governments."

Out of our three survey sites, Delhi has perhaps the least explicitly hostile environment for migrant workers, being in

11. Some of this prejudice is described in Gopalakrishnan and Chauhan (2014).

essence a city of migrants and lacking the political tradition of ethnic mobilisation that both Tamil Nadu and Uttarakhand have. But this does not preclude anti-migrant prejudice in the capital city either, perhaps best symbolised by former Chief Minister Sheila Dikshit's infamous statement that migrants were responsible for the city's increasing rape rate (Ansari 2012). Once again, our survey indicated that workers in Delhi, too, face prejudice and discrimination.

In all three locations, prejudice and chauvinistic politics targeting migrant workers share certain common characteristics. The first is the equation of migrant workers with crime. The second is the position that the state is somehow not responsible for their welfare—since they are "outsiders." Both of these intersect with the general marginalisation that targets informal sector workers. The result is a situation of multiple marginalisation and easy exploitation.

## Mobilisation Among Workers—Questions of Political Consciousness

The other key form of politicisation around migrants is the political consciousness of migrant workers themselves, and the political constraints that bind them. We can broadly divide these constraints and dynamics into two categories—those that flow from their position in the informal sector, and those that flow from their status as migrants.

### *Informalisation and Politics*

Most informal sector and daily wage work in India is characterised by certain structural features, and our survey sample was no exception. These features have been described at length elsewhere,[12] and hence are only summarised here:

- *Layers of contracting and subcontracting:* Employment is generally characterised by at least one layer of "contracting out"—in which, as in the case of small construction site, the "contract" may be taken by one of the workers themselves—and, in the case of larger projects, by several such layers. We have already seen the implications this has for the enforcement of labour law. In many cases, workers are unaware of even the name of their actual employer.
- *Impermanent and shifting types and locations of work*: Though most extreme in the context of daily wage construction work, this applies to most parts of the informal sector (as discussed in the section on our study sample).
- *Lack of security of employment:* It goes without saying that none of these occupations has any security of any kind. Daily wage work is by definition constantly in flux, while even other forms of work can be terminated at any time. Those in the construction sector face not only employment insecurity, but also loss of work as a result of the weather, illness or myriad other random factors.
- *Violence and lack of legal protection in the workplace*: It is not only labour rights that are violated in informal sector employment. Physical violence is far from uncommon, especially when workers seek redressal for their rights, such as non-payment of wages or work beyond the agreed terms of employment.

12. See the summaries contained in Gopalakrishnan and Sreenivasa (2009) and Gopalakrishnan and Sreenivasa (2010) for some of this discussion.

All this adds up to a situation characterised by three fundamental features: *atomisation, desperation* and *disorganisation*. Workers compete against one another for employment, and one of the most commonly cited complaints was that other workers were willing to work for less. Desperation emerges in the fact that no worker can be sure of their income at any time—they do not know if they will get work; if they get work, they do not know if they will get paid; and if they get paid they do not know how long their work will last. The resultant 'time horizon', as managers would be put it, is extremely short. Finally, the shifts in employers and types of work mean that there is no continuous sense of organised collective activity (unlike the 'classical' domain of a factory), and workers may find themselves working alongside new people at any time. In the case of daily wage work, the lowest layer of contracting emerges from among the workers themselves, introducing tensions and contradictions among them.

These realities makes organising of any kind—both formal, through unions, and informal, in the sense of 'spontaneous' organising—much more difficult. None of the workers in our sample in Tamil Nadu were in any trade union, or affiliated to any party. Those in Dehradun and Delhi were (64% in Delhi and 75% in Dehradun), but this was an artifact of our "snowball" survey methodology rather than any reflection of wider organisation among this class of workers.

These problems then intersect with the political realities of migration.

### *The Specifics of Migrant Marginalisation*

We noted above that migrant workers face forms of harassment, discrimination and violence that continue even after they have spent decades in their area of destination. When combined with the politics of informal work, this has specific political consequences.

The first of these is a sense of *detachment* from local struggles and local politics. This is most apparent in workers in the "first stage" of migration, as they are not necessarily committed to remaining in one location (even if they have been coming there for several years). There are thus marked differences in the political attitudes even among migrant workers, which also translate into differences between areas where migrant workers live. Areas where single young men first arrive in a city or region, for instance, have a very different response to threats of harassment or demolition than areas where workers have settled with their families. Workers respond to an atmosphere of prejudice, contempt and official indifference by withdrawing into a kind of isolated existence. This is difficult to capture in survey data, but was apparent in our discussions with our survey participants.

The second is a sense of overwhelming *marginalisation* that leads to a kind of fatalistic acceptance of a position of oppression. In our survey, in addition to our questions about discrimination, we asked about safety, and the majority of those interviewed said they do feel safe. Even 89% of those interviewed in Tamil Nadu—where 90% had said they faced discrimination and violence at the hands of the police—nevertheless said they felt 'safe.' This seems to be, as is so often the situation in India, a reflection of a deeply reduced notion of what "safety" is. Similarly, in Tamil Nadu, we noted that many of those interviewed expressed their happiness at receiving wages higher than they could at home and hence described their living conditions in Tamil Nadu initially in quite glowing terms. In all three sites, workers were more likely to deny both discrimination and violence at the first question. It was only when more specific questions were asked and discussions initiated that their experiences emerged.

In itself this second point is nothing unusual among marginalised and working class people in India. But the level of fatalism seems higher among migrant workers than among others, reflecting a sense of complete isolation and lack of options.

The third consequence is a sense of *mutual* disconnection between migrant workers, a product of the combination of the dynamics of the informal sector and the sense of lack of attachment to a particular location. This was apparent in our discussions as well as in our other experiences in Delhi and Dehradun. Mutual identification as members of either a class or a community was absent, and mutual suspicion was high. Workers saw others as competitors and even as threats to their physical safety. It is common for workers to initially attribute police violence or harassment to the actions of other migrants, saying that they give the migrant community a bad name. This sense of mutual disconnection is highest among workers in the first stage of migration, who are in a much more insecure position.

All this produces a sense of cynicism and anger that was apparent in our interviews. Workers who had not been exposed to any prior mobilisatoin were automatically deeply cynical about unions or struggles. In Delhi, even though 62% of those interviewed were affiliated to a union and all of them felt their union had been active, all the respondents (unionised or not) said that their more recent rally or protest had had no results at all.

The incorporation of these workers into the political process hence follows a very narrow and standard route (except the rare situations where a genuine union or movement organisation exists). They are mobilised by political parties through the most basic patron-client relationships, where party leaders provide a small amount of physical security—such as intervening in police harassment or sometimes stopping slum demolitions—and in exchange demand votes and other forms of political support. For instance, it is a known fact across north India that when political parties need to produce a large crowd, they approach local migrant daily wage workers and offer to pay them and provide food for them to attend. This form of clientelistic politics then becomes the basis for a cycle of dependency between politicians and workers.

Again, this is not unique to migrant workers. But the degree to which it operates among them is considerably more severe. Both parties and other forms of politics build deeper and relatively more long-term relationships, even clientelistic ones, with local and rural workers. But with these workers, relationships are transactional, cynical and often short-term.

All of this makes it difficult to organise migrant workers in 'traditional' trade union forms, which often rely on targeting a particular employer or limited group of employer for specific wage-related gains. For a class whose primary goals are not immediate wage gains but *recognition*, *inclusion* and *security*, these forms of organising offer limited gains. Successful organising of migrant workers, to the extent that it has occurred, has hence revolved around different models.

# 6

# Strategies and Ways Forward

Our study confirmed a fact that all those who work in the sector already know—that migrant workers in the informal sector are among the most marginalised and superexploited sections of Indian society. However, the specifics of this exploitation and marginalisation do offer some hints of possible ways forward.

The first point that emerges, not only from our study, but also from efforts at organising migrant workers and the authors' own experiences in this regard, is the importance of the role of the *state* in the political regime around migrant workers. Key aspects of the state's role in creating the structures of exploitation of migrant workers include:

- The structure of labour law, which specifically denies both the informal sector and migrant workers the protection of law.
- The denial of entitlements and non-implementation of welfare laws and schemes. This deprives workers of crucial economic benefits, but its impact is not limited to that. The welfare system is one of the crucial mechanisms the Indian state has for identifying, recognising and thereby *constituting* the citizenship of its residents. Denying welfare entitlements effectively *disenfranchises* migrant workers.

- The targeting of migrant workers by state agencies, above all by the police, and the manner in which this both reflects and facilitates chauvinistic politics.

This combination of factors then has three effects. It makes superexploitation possible, by rendering migrant workers into non-citizens whose wages don't need to be paid, whose work does not need to be respected, and who can be literally beaten and possibly even killed at will. It also makes chauvinistic politics both more appealing and more feasible, since migrants can be attacked with impunity and made into scapegoats for every social ill.

And thirdly, it creates the process of *disorganisation* we described above. Successful mobilisations, whether formal or informal, whether through unions or "spontaneously", whether through long politicisation or direct action, require targets against whom mobilisation can yield some kind of gain. When employers are constantly changing, and those that exist at present are immune to any action except the direct use of physical pressure or force (which in turn would result in brutal retaliation from the police), mobilisation becomes extremely difficult.

### *Ways Towards Struggles for Rights*

As a result of the above, we can suggest two primary routes that models of defending workers' rights can build on. The first is to frame demands aimed not at employers but at the state, which is the more fundamental actor in this situation. The second is to build on existing frameworks of collective identity among these workers, weak as they are.

As an example, we can look at one form of struggle that attempts to address both these requirements (disclosure: two of the researchers on this study, Shankar Gopalakrishnan and Trepan Singh Chauhan, are involved in this movement).[13] As we noted above, one of the key land uses by migrant workers are the mazdoor "chowks", or the areas where workers stand at the side of the road in the morning to be picked up for work. These spaces have no formal recognition—even though most have existed for decades—and are frequently subject to eviction and "clearing" by the police (which often consists of unauthorised lathi charges that injure workers). But chowks are not just 'markets' where workers seek work—they are also social spaces where workers may come to meet one another, to exchange notes or to socialise. They are also one of the few spaces in the city where casual workers see each other as a common *class*, even as they compete for work. In Dehradun, following a police assault on workers at the chowk in Jakhan in 2013, the union launched a mobilisation to defend the chowks and seek legal recognition of these spaces. While the legal recognition has not been granted till date, police violence against workers at chowks declined greatly after the protests, and today lathi charges are almost unknown in Dehradun.

Such struggles offer one model of mobilising migrant workers around issues that are potentially both more radical and offer more possibilities than more traditional wage demands.

As a result, models of organising migrant daily wage and casual labourers that have had some degrees of success in various parts of the country include:

- Accelerating registration under the Building Workers' Act and distribution of welfare benefits—this has been a central focus of many construction workers' unions, and since construction operates as

13. See Gopalakrishnan and Chauhan (2014) for more on this issue.

a kind of "gateway sector" for many casual labourers and migrants, this can be critical for more reasons than welfare benefits alone. It also provides security and official recognition to these workers.

- Creation of a helpline to register complaints of non-payment of wages to daily wage workers—a struggle for this has been undertaken in Dehradun for addressing the lack of legal structures and labour law for protecting the rights of casual workers.
- Separate boards for welfare benefits and payments to daily wage workers—Demands to this effect are well known from other struggles by daily wage and casual workers in states like Kerala and Maharashtra (the prototype for this law being the wage board for the *mathadi* and *hamal* workers in Maharashtra).
- Universal registration and welfare provision to migrant workers—struggles around the Unorganised Sector Workers' Act, which was eventually diluted to the point of meaninglessness, sought to mandate such a system.
- Demands for regularisation of slum housing—an issue already taken up by unions and organisations across the country.

These approaches hence address the need to tackle the structures of state function that *disorganise* workers by forcing them into a position of raw competition with one another, on the one hand, and desperate, insecure conditions of survival on the other.

These approaches are sometimes dismissed as "reformist" or "welfarist", but such analyses are misleading. As we noted above, the class position of migrant workers is characterised by structural features that make explicitly *political* demands both possible and essential. Trade union organising that assumes a particular form of labour relations —such as assuming factory or organised sector status— cannot respond to the needs of migrant workers, and indeed cannot challenge many of the more fundamental forms of labour restructuring that have been introduced by neoliberal "reforms." These forms of organising, on the other hand, can do so. In this sense they can, if seen within such a larger framework, in fact be more radical than those of older models of organising.

### State and Policy Changes

In a similar manner, those working at the policy level—or those in organisations that have reached a stage of policy negotiation—can also focus on issues of this nature rather than purely on blanket policies that for welfare or rights. Considering the utter, complete failure of laws like the Contract Labour Act, it is not enough to merely state that laws "are made and then not implemented." They are not implemented because they are structured in such a way that they will never be implemented—since they disempower precisely the people whose rights they claim to protect.

In this sense, rather than making paper promises of certain rights, policies should seek to address:

- Ease and universality of registration, in order to provide workers with rights and minimum benefits.
- Institutions ensuring that complaints of violations of rights can be easily filed and pursued.
- Institutions to decrease vulnerability in places like housing, mazdoor *chowks* and basic services.

All or any of these have the effect of increasing the security of migrant workers, and hence of increasing their ability to organise and to fight for their rights.

## Conclusion

The extraordinary superexploitation and inhuman oppression of migrant workers constitutes one of the most glaring black marks on the record of the Indian state and ruling classes since independence. These people—particularly the casual and daily wage workers who formed the focus of our study—are central to major sectors of the Indian economy, including those which are advertised as central to India's growth "boom", and yet they work in subhuman conditions with hardly any legal protection for their rights.

This superexploitation has its roots in fundamentally political causes—an institutional and state structure that disenfranchises and disorganises migrant workers. This in turn has a direct impact on the choices available to them and the politics with which those choices are approached. Organising to challenge these limits and to build new forms of labour relations in these sectors is central to addressing the injustices of India's economy and to building a more just, more productive and more *human* polity in this country.

# References


Agrawal, Tushar, and S. Chandrasekhar. 2015. "Short Term Migrants in India: Characteristics, Wages and Work Transition." Indira Gandhi Institute of Development Research. http://www.igidr.ac.in/pdf/publication/WP-2015-07.pdf.

Ansari, Javed. 2012. "Sheila Dikshit Blames Migrants, Porous Border for Delhi Rapes." *India Today*, 12 April.

Chauhan, Trepan Singh, and Shankar Gopalakrishnan. 2014. "Violence Against Women Unorganised Sector Workers in the City of Dehradun." Social Research Collective. http://srcindia.wordpress.com.

Deshingkar, Priya, and Daniel Start. 2003. "Seasonal Migration for Livelihoods in India: Coping, Accumulation and Exclusion." Overseas Development Institute. http://www.odi.org.uk/resources/docs/74.pdf.

Dutta, Madhumita. 2012. "Come South, Young Man, but Here Be Dragons." *The Hindu*, 9 March.

Gopalakrishnan, Shankar, and Trepan Singh Chauhan. 2014. "Struggles Over Class and Space in an Indian City." *Economic and Political Weekly* 49 (26-27).

Gopalakrishnan, Shankar, and Priya Sreenivasa. 2009. *The Political Economy of Migration*. New Delhi: Aakar Books.

———. 2010. *Strategies and Tools for Organising Migrant Workers*. Aakar Books.

Gopalakrishnan, Shankar, Trepan Singh Chauhan, and Ramendra Kumar. 2014. "Domestic Workers in Delhi and Dehradun: Oppression in the Space of the Home." KISLAY Social Research Collective. https://srcindia.files.wordpress.com/

2015/01/domestic_workers_study_dec_2014_final.pdf.

Philip, Christin Mathew. 2016. "Tamil Nadu Now Home to 1 Million Migrant Workers: Study." *Times of India*, 5 February.

Rao, J. Mohan. 1999. "Agrarian Power and Unfree Labour." *Journal of Peasant Studies* 26 (2).

Ray, Shantanu Guha, and Shoma Chaudhury. 2008. "'My Vision Is to Get 85 Percent of India into Cities'." *Tehelka*. http://archive.tehelka.com/story_main39.asp?filename=Ne310508cover_story.asp.

Shah, Alpa, and Barbara Harriss-White. 2011. "Resurrecting Scholarship on Agrarian Transformations." *Economic and Political Weekly* XLVI (39): 13–18.

Sharma, Amrita, and Rajiv Khandewal. 2014. "The Invisible City Makers: Of Migration and Migrant Workers in India." *Cafe Dissensus*, 1 August. https://cafedissensus.com/2014/08/01/the-invisible-city-makers-of-migration-and-migrant-workers-in-india/.

Srivastava, Ravi, and S.K. Sasikumar. 2003. "An Overview of Migration in India, Its Impacts and Key Issues." Migration, Development and Pro-Poor Policy Choices in Asia. Department for International Development. https://www.eldis.org/vfile/upload/1/document/0903/Dhaka_CP_2.pdf.

Upadhyay, Kavita. 2014. "Migration Leaves Behind 'Ghost Villages' in Uttarakhand." *The Hindu*, 10 November. http://www.thehindu.com/news/national/other-states/migration-leaves-behind-ghost-villages-in-uttarakhand/article6580917.ece.

Warrier, Shobha. 2012. "'In Tamil Nadu, the Administration Itself Is Targeting People'." *Rediff.com*, 24 April.